PRESIDENT
TRUMP

*How Donald Trump's Proposed
Policies will Shape the USA and
World in 2017 and Beyond*

TONY ROBSON

President Trump

Copyright © 2017

All rights reserved.

Table of Contents

Introduction

Thank you for downloading President Trump: How Donald Trump's Proposed Policies will Shape the USA and World in 2017 and Beyond! I hope you enjoy reading it!

A Presidential candidate's success is an homage to his efficient campaigning and his proficient governing plans and policies. President-elect Trump defied all expectations of critics and experts when his candidacy reigned supreme in the much maligned and controversial Election campaign of 2016. While his campaigning was considered unorthodox and contentious, his presidential policies are an appealing proposition to a majority of the American people; which helped sway the election in his favor, another they are also considered very dangerous by another conflicted and fearful majority.

With President-elect soon taking the helm of the most powerful position in the world, this book discusses in detail the policies Trump has promised to strive to implement as President, and the affects they will have in their subsequent fields. From his famous "Build the Wall!" movement, his immigration policies, to his position on the NATO and Nuclear policies; this book explores all possible result and affects Trumps policies might implicate.

CHAPTER I
Foreign Policy

A turbulent campaign, one that confined change in perspective, enticed conflict and made us question our unity as a nation; the Presidential Election 2016 was one for the ages. It, not only changed our perception on politics, but our views of the perception of other people, constantly revealing different aspects of other people's lives that we thought we had forgotten. It revealed those people as a group that had been forgotten, outcast of the political viewpoint, ignored by the national elite. However, Presidential Republican candidate Donald Trump gave them a forsaken voice, which they had been calling out for years. He gave them leadership, attention and listened to them. While most of the mainstream media and communal thinking had thought this forgotten group of people was apparently minimal, it turned out to be more than a surprise for them. Coupled with the fact that Donald Trump's Presidential opponent was a rather scandalous one; due to her investigations by the FBI, Trump managed to sway the heads of undecided voters as well. The result was an overwhelming turnout and a rather surprising victory on Election night. While many were shocked by the result, the victory is credited to Trump's immaculate campaign trail and the way he swayed the undecided voters; something that didn't turn up in the previously suggested polls. An inexperienced, controversial and a surprising candidate had won the Election as per his due diligence, and hard-work. The result in the end might be surprising, but credit to where it's due.

The surprise wasn't just among the domestic arrears; where Election results sparked mass protests in the streets of the United States as people rejected the result, it was surprising for other nations as well. While other countries may not be overly concerned about the Presidential Election in comparison to previous elections, there may be some circumstances where the results of the election might be a bit worrying for some. Donald Trump has made some statements and proposals on foreign policy that might be conferred as ethically, morally and intellectually inept. But his demeanor as a businessman; a demeanor that he has exemplified the image of to his voters as an example of his business empire, his moral ethic that America should get something in return might be one that is beneficial to the United States. But in lieu of that assessment, it seems to distract from the larger picture, which might cause unintentional drawbacks and possible world disasters.

While most of Donald Trump's statements give out an incoherent and unsubstantial outlook on the world and its workings, he actually has a very clear view, and that view is transactional; if you pay America, America will help you. It can be clearly recognized in his Presidential debate with Hillary Clinton in which he said, "We are being ripped off, we're defending other countries. We're spending a fortune and they have the bargain of the century". It is prominent that his views expand that of a normal bureaucratic outlook, but rather a back and forth kind, where the services that America shall provide are only monetarily available. And because of this, the benefit of America is put first. But the view-point of having America's benefit is of a more controlling perspective than that of peaceful agreement. Addressing the Conservative Political Action Conference back in 2013, when Donald Trump said that he got to know that America was going into Iraq for the oil. And at other instances he uttered the desire to go into Iraq and 'hit the oil' and 'bomb the oil'. While we could theoretically do it, but the collateral damage and possible conflict would be a terrifying prospect. While he does give the reasoning that the oil would be a way to pay ourselves back, it gives an imperialistic form of governance which always leads to bad things

NATO & Russia

The constant issue that embarks the US in a dangerous tussle with its allies is actually an imperative one. The issue that all NATO countries promised to pay a certain amount of GDP to its defense, but no country other than US is fulfilling that promise. And when Trump calls out on this issue, that it's an expensive issue and America should do something about it, he is correct. The United States, not being supported by other allies in the fulfilling of this promise, makes it difficult for US to enhance foreign relations. But while the solution is a given that there should be an outcry where America should ask the NATO countries to pay up, he chooses to go on another extreme. He takes it to the part that if any other country invades another NATO country, America will rethink its position in aiding the country. This scenario would be a complete violation of the Section 5 of the NATO Charter, where it is emphasized that if one of the NATO member countries is attacked, other 27 countries shall come to its defense. Hence if this charter is violated, it would cause serious damage to foreign relations and the world order as a whole. Most of these countries signed this charter NATO charter, mainly to keep Russia at bay.

This move would play right into Russia's hands, as for the past 20 years, Putin and the Russian administration have aimed this as their top strategic goal, to weaken NATO. And Donald Trump's longing intention of improving relations with Russia provides incentive to this issue. Donald Trump continues to defend Putin's position and portrays him as a model leader as he defines him as effective, efficient and popular; regardless of his outrageous tactics in Syria, Crimea and constant support of Assad.

Nuclear Weapons

One of the many successful things the foreign policy of recent governments and presidents, whether they be Republican or Democrat, it's the constant will to strive in keeping Nuclear weapons out of countries' hands. And in turn, help in increasing diplomatic relations by striving for peace-keeping policies, something that has been the constant aim of the United Nations. Something similar has been attained with Eastern Asian countries such as Japan and South Korea. United States has successfully retained an agreement between the two Asian countries in limiting nuclear warhead production by the help of the United States. While increasing diplomatic relations by promising nuclear protection by the United States, if a situation of a nuclear attack arises from North Korea. This keeps the subsequent countries in the nuclear umbrella of the United States; which has the largest nuclear arsenal in the world, hence allows the United States to keep military bases in the countries and receive diplomatic perks. It is an agreement that had been lauded at the Nuclear Summit 2016, as an integral step of diplomacy in Barack Obama's two terms as President.

However, President-elect Trump's constant monetary precedent may change the situation in the region and may bring tyranny if this deal is brought into any danger. While Trump's demand of monetary pleasures in exchange for nuclear protection, he doesn't seem to realize the diplomatic relations may tend to profit the United States. And if this deal is annulled, there would be massive instability in the region of Eastern Asia, may give incentive to North Korea in order to break it's ceasefire with the South and hence also attack Japan. And with North Korea openly declaring war against the United States, Trump might need to take their war declaration if such a dire situation takes place

ISIS

During the Presidential Election and the subsequently held debates, an offensive tactic adopted by President-elect Trump; Secretary Hillary Clinton, was that Donald Trump doesn't have a quantitative plan to defeat the ever-present danger that is ISIS. However, Trump has long blamed his opponent, Democrat and former Secretary of State Hillary Clinton, and current President Barack Obama for allowing ISIS to establish itself as a global menace. "We cannot let this evil continue. Nor can we let the hateful ideology of radical Islam — its oppression of women, gays, children and nonbelievers — be allowed to reside or spread within our own countries," Trump said in an August speech. "We will defeat radical Islamic terrorism, just as we have defeated every threat we have faced in every age before."

Trump has subsequently proposed a thorough plan in order to defeat this menace that threatens US and its allies. First, Trump will work the U.S.' connections in the Middle East, calling on Israel, Jordan and Egypt to battle ISIS. Trump said he thinks Americans could also team up with Russia and the North Atlantic Treaty Organization. Together, the coalition will coordinate aggressive military missions to curb ISIS' influence, limit their funding, share intelligence and take down their propaganda troops. Next, he plans to engage in what he called ideological warfare. "Just as we won the Cold War, in part, by exposing the evils of communism and the virtues of free markets, so too must we take on the ideology of radical Islam," he said in his speech, outlining his proposals to condemn practices like honor killings and other kinds of oppression. Trump will put together a commission that teaches people to recognize radical Muslims and disable groups that make it possible.

Finally, he will temporarily stop immigration from certain countries.

"We should only admit into this country those who share our values and respect our people," he said. "I will ask the State Department and the Department of Homeland Security to identify a list of regions where adequate screening cannot take place. We will stop processing visas from those areas until such time as it is deemed safe to resume based on new circumstances or new procedures."

While some might perceive it to be a radical plan in order to defeat ISIS, but the immigration amendments and social warfare maybe directed towards an immigrant and non-white secular groups within the United States, as described by most political analysts. This would in turn entice the extremist thinking of some groups that would think of it as a way to exploit and harass certain immigrant and Muslim groups. And the pausing of immigration to the United States would be a way to stop the recent migration of Middle Eastern Arabs to the west when they try to get out unstable regions in the Middle East, with countries such as Syria and Libya etc.

CHAPTER 2
Build the Wall!

"Build that wall! Build that wall!" was a favorite chant at Trump campaign rallies. As a real estate developer, this would be his most impressive construction job. As he said early in his campaign, "I would build a great wall, and nobody builds walls better than me, believe me, and I build them very inexpensively."

Critics were as dismissive of Trump's wall as they were of Trump as a presidential candidate. The wall proposal, they said, was nothing more than a political fantasy. But under President Trump, the wall will not only be for real, but it may be one of his biggest political successes. Here's how.

Whatever is built or is already there, Trump will call it a wall

Words matter. When one thinks of a wall, one thinks of something solid — which, no doubt, is part of its enormous political appeal for Trump supporters. But the term "wall" is actually surprisingly fuzzy. The various Oxford dictionary definitions of a wall include "any high vertical surface, especially one that is imposing in scale." That broad definition would seem to leave Trump a lot of wiggle room. It is important to remember that Trump's predecessors carefully avoided calling any new border barriers a "wall." Before Trump, the term was politically taboo, viewed as sending the wrong message to Mexico and to the world. When Pat Buchanan ran for president in 1996, he proposed building a "sea wall" to stop the "tidal wave" of illegal immigration across the border — and was dismissed as an extremist and ostracized by the Republican Party.

But times have changed. Trump broke the taboo. His fans have loved him for it. So regardless of what Trump ends up building, calling it a "wall" will sound like something new and make his followers cheer.

Much of the wall has already been built

Since the early 1990s, politicians of all stripes have scrambled to show their commitment to border security. During that time, annual federal funding for border and immigration control mushroomed from $1.5 billion to $19.5 billion. According to one estimate, Washington spends $5 billion more on border and immigration control than for all other federal law enforcement combined.

And the result? Hundreds of miles of metal barriers have gone up. Technologies initially developed for the military have been adapted for border enforcement. A fleet of manned and unmanned aircrafts have been deployed to monitor from the air. Thousands of new agents have been hired. The size of the Border Patrol doubled in the 1990s and has more than doubled again since the beginning of the century, from about 4,000 personnel to more than 21,000.

This massive enforcement buildup has been lethal for many migrants trying to cross, with thousands of deaths to date, while enriching the smugglers on whom migrants must rely. As I showed in my book "Border Games: Policing the U.S. Mexico Divide," it has been politically rewarding for both Democrats and Republicans alike. Trump is simply taking it to the next level.

Trump has dismissed the current state of border security as "a joke," but he'll soon find that the bipartisan border policing boom started in the 1990s will be crucial to keeping his wall pledge. Trump's plan calls for a wall that covers 1,000 miles of the nearly 2,000-mile-long border — with natural obstacles covering the remainder. Nearly 700 miles of various types of border fencing are already in place, and portions of it very much look like a formidable metal wall. It is hard to imagine Trump tearing all that fencing up and starting from scratch.

What's much more realistic is that Trump will simply add more miles of fencing; reinforce existing fencing in key, visible places; and deploy even more border guards, stadium lighting, and the latest high-tech detection and surveillance equipment. The newest, tallest part of the Trump Wall — probably erected at one of the most visible, urban spots on the border — would be an effective backdrop for the president's celebratory news conference announcing its construction.

In the end, Trump's wall is likely to be the latest addition to the border barrier-building frenzy first launched by President Bill Clinton, greatly expanded by George W. Bush and continued by Obama. But Trump will take full ownership of it as the only president willing to actually call it a wall. It will not stop migrants from entering the country illegally — going over, under or around it, with many of them dying in the process. But when Trump supporters grumble that the wall is too porous, Trump will no doubt promise to make the wall even longer, taller and stronger in his second term.

However, there are some instances and indications that show that this precedent might be exceeding than first proposed. Three days after Trump, in an appearance on "60 Minutes," indicated he might build a fence instead (though in "certain areas, a wall is more appropriate"), congressional Republicans are hedging on whether they'll support building the border wall, suggesting it may turn out to be some combination of wall, fencing, and "invisible fence" technology such as patrolling by drones.

And surrogates for Trump have been suggesting that the wall might end up being more of a metaphor for enhancing border security than an actual bricks-and-mortar barrier. Utah's Orrin Hatch, the most senior GOP senator, said Trump was "serious about having a way of keeping people out who shouldn't be in our country," but that the idea of a wall would have to be "re-evaluated."

"I think the best way to say it is, do whatever it takes to secure the border," Senate Judiciary Chairman Chuck Grassley (R-Iowa) said in an interview to POLITICO.

Trump ally Newt Gingrich said the president-elect's pledge to get Mexico to pay for the border wall was a mere "campaign device." The former House speaker might not have been speaking for Trump by suggesting Mexico would never pay for the wall, but few believe it ever would.

And Dr. Ben Carson, Trump's former primary-rival-turned-surrogate, told conservatives on a conference call this week that what Trump "really wants to do is secure the border," The Wall Street Journal reported. He added: "You can rest assured that those principles will be followed, but it may not necessarily be the exact letter."

Trump immigration adviser Kris Kobach told Reuters that the administration could reallocate funds from the Department of Homeland Security budget and apply them to construction of the wall, a move that would bypass Congress and get the project off to a quick start. But continued construction would require congressional appropriations in future years.

Many congressional Republicans favor a simpler idea: abandon the idea of building a massive wall and focus instead on other ways to increase border security.

"I think you're going to find some areas where a wall would never work, and I think everybody's always understood that," said Sen. Mike Rounds of South Dakota. "In other areas, it might be something like a fence. But in all cases, what we're talking about is securing the southern border." Part of the challenge, Rounds said, will be to figure out the "most modern approach" to border security. Rep. Pete Sessions, a

Republican who represents a district in suburban Dallas, said the wall could be thought of as "an analogy" for fences and drone surveillance. "We're going to defend our sovereignty and our immigration policy."

Sen. Jeff Flake (R-Ariz.), who feuded with Trump during the campaign season, said he hadn't followed developments about the wall but that he supports Trump's plan to deport immigrants who have committed crimes. "If he deports those with criminal records," Flake said, "he'll get no argument from me."

CHAPTER 3

Immigration Policy

During Mitt Romney's campaign for President, in 2012, he claimed that he could solve the political conundrum of immigration reform by getting undocumented immigrants to "self-deport" from the United States en masse. He was roundly mocked for the idea. Why would millions of people voluntarily leave a country they'd long considered home? His suggestion, though, was hardly a flub—it was meant to be a serious threat. For Kris Kobach, the adviser who sold Romney on the concept, the eventuality of widespread self-deportation was entirely feasible. The government simply had to make life so unrelentingly difficult for immigrants that they'd have no other choice.

Kobach, who has been the Kansas secretary of state since 2011, is advising President-elect Donald Trump during the transition, and he appears to be a candidate for a top post in the incoming Administration. Kobach met with Trump in Bedminster, New Jersey, to "discuss border security, international terrorism, and reforming federal bureaucracy," according to an official statement. If Trump intends to expel the country's undocumented immigrants—one of the core pledges of his campaign—Kobach is a natural ally. For more than a decade, he has been the Republican Party's anointed ideas man for hard-line immigration policies. A press photograph taken of Trump and Kobach together after their meeting Sunday captured a hint of what might be in store. In plain view, Kobach held a memo detailing his "Strategic Plan" for the "Department of Homeland Security." Several policy proposals were exposed to the camera: a national registry to help "bar entry of potential terrorists"; "extreme vetting" for "high-risk aliens"; construction plans for the "rapid build" of the border wall.

Kobach is fifty years old, and is a graduate of Harvard, Yale Law School, and Oxford, where he received a doctorate in political science. While serving in the Justice Department after 9/11, he helped create a national registry to track immigrants from countries with a "high risk" of terrorism—an effort that resulted in zero terrorism prosecutions but put nearly fourteen thousand people in deportation proceedings. In 2003, Kobach left the federal government. He taught law at the University of Missouri-Kansas City, but he wanted greater influence as an advocate, so he also took a position as a lawyer with an arm of the Federation for American Immigration Reform (fair), an organization that the Southern Poverty Law Center has designated a "hate group." (Fair has disputed the categorization.)

Over the next several years, Kobach used fair as the base of operations for a nationwide campaign to make life miserable for immigrants. In California, he appeared before the state's Supreme Court to argue against a law that made college affordable for undocumented students known as Dreamers, who arrived in the U.S. as children. On his home turf, in

Kansas, he opposed granting in-state college tuition to the children of undocumented immigrants. In Arizona, he argued on behalf of a county that sought to criminalize immigrants as felons for "smuggling" themselves across the border.

The federal government sets immigration-enforcement policy, but Kobach's approach was to make municipal and state governments vehicles for draconian new initiatives. In recent years, he was involved in either drafting or defending sweeping anti-immigrant legislation passed in Arizona, Georgia, Alabama, South Carolina, and Utah, as well as local ordinances in cities and towns in Pennsylvania, Texas, and Nebraska. These measures all relied on a legal theory known as "inherent authority," which Kobach has used to argue that local and state officials have the power to enforce national immigration laws if they believe the federal government has been too lax.

When it came to making the case for the measures in court, however, Kobach lost much more often than he won. In Hazleton, Pennsylvania, he argued in defense of an ordinance passed in 2006 that made it illegal for local landlords to rent to undocumented immigrants. Still, Kobach's long game may have had less to do with creating legal precedent than it did with sowing social discord. According to the Migration Policy Institute, between July, 2006, and July, 2007, a hundred and eighteen proposals similar to Hazleton's came up for consideration in towns across the country. This was how self-deportation was supposed to become a reality—if you put immigrants in the center of a raging populist debate at every level of state and local government, life got ugly for them. The policy fight in Hazleton prompted a number of violent incidents, including threats made against the town's immigrant community. Rocks were thrown through the windows of stores owned by immigrants. Eventually, the Justice Department had to get involved.

Kobach is best known for co-authoring the country's harshest anti-immigration law, Arizona's Senate Bill 1070, which passed in 2010 and inspired "copycat" bills in five other states. The law was an open invitation to racial profiling by local and state police: it required law-enforcement officers to ask individuals about their immigration status if there was a "reasonable suspicion" that they might be undocumented. The law also made it a crime for an undocumented immigrant to work anywhere in the state, or to go anywhere without papers. "Arizona really has been a trailblazer in discouraging illegal immigration," Kobach told the Arizona *Republic*. When, a year later, Alabama passed a similar bill, Kobach took another victory lap. "Without question, Alabama's House Bill 56 is the most comprehensive anti-illegal-immigration state law ever drafted," he said.

In 2012, the Supreme Court dismantled much of Arizona's law, and the states that had followed with legislation of their own lost parallel fights in the courts. Afterward, Kobach moved away from immigration policy and spent a few years fighting the spectre of voter fraud, another right-wing obsession.

Trump's election has revived Kobach's anti-immigration agenda. Earlier this month, in an interview on CNN, Kobach defended the President-elect's recent promise to deport two to three million "criminals" upon taking office. "Criminal" is a term that Kobach has long tried to blur into total ambiguity in the context of immigration reform. On CNN, he argued that the incoming Administration would need to expand the definition of "criminal" to include people who have been arrested but not yet convicted. (Trump cited two to three million people as candidates for immediate deportation, but, according to the National Immigration Law Center, only about eight hundred thousand undocumented immigrants have been convicted of crimes in the U.S., many of them for nonviolent offenses like minor immigration violations.) Those who've followed Kobach's career over the years recognized this approach. The whole premise of the Arizona law was to allow the flimsiest pretext of lawbreaking to trigger an arrest—and for that arrest to then open the door to a full investigation of an individual's immigration status. According to Vivek Malhotra, the former director of civil and human rights at the Ford Foundation, the Trump Administration "looks like it will go back to this notion that people can be absorbed into the deportation process merely by being arrested. You'll be criminalizing huge swaths of immigrant communities by targeting them for arrest." In the photograph that was taken after Kobach's meeting with Trump, one phrase from his memo stood out: the definition of "criminal alien" as "any alien *arrested* for any crime."

Kobach has vocally backed Trump's plans to build a border wall, and he has not only supported the idea of creating a national registry for Muslims living in the U.S. but advocated for it on the grounds that the Japanese internment during the Second World War is a legitimizing precedent. Two days after the election, he told the Los Angeles *Times*, "There is a vast potential to increase the level of deportations without adding personnel." In the interview, he fantasized about returning to a time like the final two years of the George W. Bush Administration, when workplace raids were routine and immigrants were hounded daily for their papers. Worse may be yet to come. Until now, Kobach's extremism has been confined to the state level. Soon, he may have the power of the federal government behind him.

However, these immigration reforms could seriously damage the economic boost proposition that Trump has made to the American people. He promised long-term economic growth that would exceed at a rate of 4 percent per year. Most economists think America's potential growth is only about 2 percent, and most agree the best way to make it higher is to get more people working and make those workers more productive. Stimulating the economy with government spending or tax cuts will only boost short-term growth and cause inflation. But right now, getting more people into the labor force is a challenge. For one, it means fighting a demographic tide.

"We have a huge wave of baby-boom era people retiring," says Robert J. Gordon, an economist at Northwestern University and author of *The Rise and Fall of American Growth*. "Right now, we've got a shortage of construction workers. We've got a shortage of long-distance truck drivers. We've got a shortage of many kinds of skilled workers needed to work in manufacturing". Gordon says bringing immigrants into the workforce is the best way to deal with this mass retirement of baby boomers.

In the past couple of decades, half the growth in the labor force has come from immigration. But,

Gordon points out; Trump has said he will deport millions of immigrants.

"They're called illegal immigrants, and they're here illegally," Trump said in an interview with CNN. "They're going to have to go, and they're going to have to come back in legally, and otherwise, we don't have a country."

Stephen Moore, who has advised Trump on his economic growth policy, says Trump isn't against immigration, just illegal immigration. Personally, Moore says he believes even some of those workers who are in the country illegally shouldn't be deported. "People who are in this country, are working, and productive Americans who are contributing, I personally would not like to see those people deported," says Moore, who is also an economic consultant with Freedom Works, the grass-roots organization that helped launch the Tea Party. He also argues that a faster growing economy will not only provide jobs for the unemployed but will attract others back into the labor force, including some retirees. Most economists are skeptical that could provide enough workers to get to a 4 percent growth rate.

In terms of making workers more productive, Moore says big tax cuts for businesses will boost investment in new equipment and technologies, such as autonomous vehicles and artificial intelligence. "We could see very rapid rises in the productivity that ... is a key part to making growth possible," Moore says. But Gordon, who has studied innovation, believes it will be several decades before those two technologies have much impact on U.S. productivity. And he notes that neither the big Reagan tax cuts nor the big Bush tax cuts boosted U.S. productivity.

Thus, in terms of keeping his policy of deportation, Trump threatens to violate some laws and amendments that were made in order to satisfy human rights protection that may protect those people from deportation. According to the administration's plan for its first 100 days in office, the President-elect will terminate the Deferred Action for Childhood Arrivals program (DACA) originally created by an executive order from President Obama in 2012.

Through DACA, individuals who came to this country as children, through no fault of their own, and met certain requirements are protected from deportation and are allowed the opportunity to work, study, and serve in the military.

If Trump follows through on his promise and terminates the program, it will have an immediate negative impact on approximately 800,000 individuals and their families, while adversely impacting the U.S. economy. LULAC is gratified by the effort in the Senate to save DACA through the introduction of the BRIDGE Act, the Bar Removal of Immigrants Who Dream and Grow the Economy Act.

Senate Minority Whip Dick Durbin (D-IL) and Senator Lindsey Graham (R-SC) introduced the BRIDGE Act recently, which would provide three years of protection to individuals who came to United States as children and allow them to continue to work hard, study, and serve in the military. The statute is designed to retain the status quo for participants in the DACA program who would otherwise be forced back into the shadows with the discontinuation of the program. Like DACA, provisional status will provide an opportunity for approximately 800,000 people to live the American dream.

Programs that offer provisional status like DACA and the BRIDGE Act are also beneficial to the American economy. The Congressional Budget Office has outlined the economic benefits of DACA to include raising the level of the U.S. GDP by $90 billion over the next ten years. In addition, the U.S. labor force would expand by nearly 150,000 workers; productivity of American workers would increase; the average wages for U.S.-born workers would increase by $170 billion; and federal deficits would see a reduction of $25 billion during the same 10-year period.

American values also speak in favor of the continuation of the DACA program. This group of individuals came to this country as children through no fault of their own. This is the only country they know, and all they ask for is an opportunity to live the American dream. These young immigrants are not criminals and are not a drain on U.S. taxpayers. To target these immigrants for deportation through the termination of the DACA program would be inconsistent with our values. It would result in families being torn apart and send a clear message that this is a country with opportunity for some, but not all Americans.

LULAC commends senators Durbin and Graham for recognizing the plight of these young people. The BRIDGE Act is a significant step in the right direction, but much more needs to be done, as it would only provide temporary relief. LULAC, with its partner organizations, will work to push for the passage of the BRIDGE Act to protect the 800,000 young people participating in DACA and will continue to fight for comprehensive solutions to our deeply flawed immigration system.

CHAPTER 4

Economic Policy

Many Americans have grown anxious that the economy hasn't lived up to its promise over the past 15 years of creating job growth that provides upward mobility and broadly shared prosperity. Instead, the nation has gone through two recessions marked by bubbles—one in the stock market and the other in housing—that were followed by recoveries in which economic growth returned but job growth lagged. Laying out a vision for how to restore widespread job and income gains is shaping up to be the top priority of the incoming president.

Mr. Trump has eschewed the sunny optimism of past Republican presidents by warning that the nation faces an almost irreversible economic decline. He has published plans for large tax cuts, reducing regulation and renegotiating trade agreements. He has provided fewer specifics about how his plans to curb immigration and to slash imports would create new jobs. Mr. Trump has promised a big boost in spending on defense and infrastructure while cutting the budgets for nondefense programs, though these include several areas such as veterans' health care and border security, where Mr. Trump has promised more spending. He has also promised not to touch popular benefit programs such as Social Security and Medicare, which account for a rising share of public spending and, as such, have been a ripe target of conservatives for decades.

On November 22, Trump promised to make the following Executive Orders. First, withdraw from the Trans-Pacific Partnership. He will replace it with a series of bilateral agreements that protect American jobs. That means eleven new agreements with the other signatories.

Second, cancel restrictions on shale oil, clean coal, and other energy production. Third, any federal agency that proposes a new regulation must identify two existing ones that will be eliminated.

Fourth, ask the Defense Department to develop a plan to protect the nation's infrastructure from cyber-attacks. Fifth, ask the Labor Department to identify any abuse of the nation's visa program.

Sixth, propose a five-year ban on executive officials becoming lobbyists. (This was also proposed by Obama during his 2008 campaign.) There will be a lifetime ban for any executive lobbying on behalf of another country.

Trump has the support of the Republican-controlled Congress. That makes it more likely his other measures will get passed.

"5-Part Tax Plan"

Eliminate the marriage penalty, the Alternative Minimum Tax, and the inheritance tax. Quadruple the standard deduction. Trump also added a childcare deduction. It would allow parents to deduct the average cost of childcare expenses.

Simplify tax preparation by reducing the current seven tax brackets to three.

Lower the maximum small business and corporate tax rate from 38 percent to 15 percent.

Get corporations to bring money back into the United States. Keep companies in this country. The United States is the highest taxed nation in the world. He would get the right people into the room, and get all to agree how to do it. The effective tax rate is only 15 percent. That's because most corporations have figured out how to avoid it. Nearly half pay no taxes at all since they pass those taxes to their shareholders. A lower corporate tax rate would increase profits without necessarily creating new jobs. That's because supply-side economics doesn't work at today's relatively low tax rates.

The taxes for the rich would go up somewhat. If I increase it on the wealthy, they're still going to pay less than they pay now. Trump has given conflicting statements on how his tax plan will affect high-income taxpayers (the top 20 percent). They would receive a 9.5 percent decrease in the tax rate. Trump would offset the tax cuts by eliminating loopholes, but he isn›t specific. The Tax Policy Center says his plan would add almost $1 trillion a year to the debt. That›s because capital gains tax cuts stimulate investment more than they do economic growth. Low-income taxpayers spend a greater proportion of their income, boosting Gross Domestic Product. Trump only gives the middle class a 4.9 percent increase in after-tax incomes.

End tax deferral on the $5 trillion in corporate cash held abroad. Allow a one-time repatriation that will be taxed 10 percent. Eliminate loopholes available to the very rich and corporations, such as the exemption on life insurance interest. Steepen the curve of the Personal Exemption Phase-out and the Pease Limitation on itemized deductions. Phase in a cap on business interest expenses.

Eliminate the "carried interest" deduction. It allows managers of hedge funds and private equity funds to be taxed at the capital gains tax rate (15 percent) instead of the income tax rate (39.6 percent).

"Cut Government Spending"

Make the U.S. military so strong no one will mess with us. Get more equipment. Bomb ISIS and send troops to Syria. Cancel Iran nuclear deal. Use Russia as an ally in Syria. Use waterboarding. Use military force against terrorists' families. Oppose

Iraq war. In a November 22 interview with the New York Times, Trump said he no longer supports waterboarding. He based his change of heart on a conversation with retired Marine Corps General James Mattis. He also said he might appoint his son-in-law, Jared Kushner, as a special envoy to broker peace between the Israelis and Palestinians.

Cut defense spending, but 3 percent of GNP for military spending is too low, it should be 6.5 percent. U.S. military spending is almost $800 billion a year. It's larger than anything other government expenditure except Social Security at $967 billion. It's bigger than the deficit of $503 billion. It's greater than those of the next ten largest spenders combined. It's four times larger than China's military budget of $216 billion. It's almost ten times bigger than Russia's budget of just $84.5 billion.

Reform the Veteran's Administration. Give veterans vouchers to use either with the VA or their own doctor. That competition would give the VA an incentive to improve service. The VA would provide transitional benefits, such as business loans, job training, and placement services, to help

veterans find jobs. **Increase funding for battle-related mental and chronic illness. Add OBGYN and other women's health services to every VA hospital. Fire corrupt VA executives. Change the culture of the VA to reduce inefficiencies.** These programs would work and are sorely needed. The VA budget ($75.1 billion) is only 10 percent of total military spending. Many vets are traumatized and don›t receive the care they need. As a result, ten percent of the homeless populations are veterans who suffer from Post-Traumatic Stress Disorder or other war-related injuries.

Update medical technology. That›s already happened. It›s one of the three largely unknown benefits of Obamacare.

Reduce the deficit by cutting waste. Trump would have to cut $500 billion in waste to eliminate the current budget deficit. That›s a 12 percent cut in the $4.147 trillion budget he will inherit from President Obama. As any business owner knows, a 12 percent cut is doable but extremely painful.

Eliminate the Department of Education and the Environmental Protection Administration. That might save $69.4 billion for Education, unless Trump reprogrammed the funds for education block grants for the states, as he mentioned elsewhere. Defunding the EPA would only save $8.3 billion and who would enforce the existing laws?

Keep existing Medicare and Social Security benefits intact. These benefits were created by prior Acts of Congress and cannot be changed by a President. Social Security is self-funded until 2035. Medicare is only 53 percent self-funded. These two programs cost $1.565 trillion, or 38 percent of total spending.

"Repeal Obamacare"

Allow health insurance companies to operate across states lines. Remove the mandate to buy insurance. Allow tax deduction for health insurance premiums and Health Savings Accounts. Expand Medicaid to all states by making it a block grant program. Allow consumers to purchase drugs overseas. Offer a universal "market-based" plan that would provide a range of choices similar to the Federal Employees Health Benefits Program.

Trump›s plan is what Obama initially proposed, and Congress rejected. For more, see Obama›s Original Health Care Reform Plan.

"Smart Trade, Not Stupid Trade"

Do a better job of negotiating trade agreements. China taxes our exports, but we don't tax its exports. That›s true to some extent. China requires American companies to set up factories to hire and train local workers before they can sell to its market. The United States could easily do the same thing.

Renegotiate NAFTA with smart and cunning people. If Trump re-opens negotiations on NAFTA, the Mexican government would immediately require that the United States allow Mexican trucks on its roads. That was promised in the first NAFTA agreement but withdrawn by Congress. Mexico is in much better economic shape now than when the three countries first negotiated NAFTA. For that reason, a new agreement would be worse for the United States, no matter how smart and cunning Trump›s people are.

Label China a currency manipulator. Trump claims that China artificially undervalues its currency, the Yuan, by 15 percent to 40 percent. Part of China's cost advantage is its cheaper standard of living that allows lower wages. Trump ignores that. He incorrectly rails against the Yuan's fixed exchange rate that's pegged to the dollar. In 2000, the Yuan *was* undervalued by 30 percent. But a lot has changed since then. First, former Treasury Secretary Hank Paulson convinced the People›s Bank of China (PBOC) to increase the Yuan's value against the dollar. It increased 2-3 percent annually between 2000 and 2013. Second, the dollar has strengthened by 25 percent since 2014, taking the Chinese Yuan with it. Now China›s products cost that much more than its Southeast Asian competitors. In August 2015, the PBOC began to carefully let the Yuan/dollar exchange rate float in the free market. The Yuan immediately plummeted. If the Yuan were undervalued, as Trump claims, it would have risen instead. Now, China›s central bank is forced to take extreme steps to keep it propped up. That›s why many economists now think

China's currency is over-valued, not under-valued as Trump claims.

Impose countervailing duties on all imports from China. The United States imports $481.9 billion in consumer electronics, clothing, and machinery from China. A lot of those "imports" are from U.S. corporations that send raw materials to China, and ship them back when they are completed. Trump's tariffs would reduce profits for these American firms and raise prices for American consumers. China might retaliate, raising its tariffs on imports from U.S. companies.

Hit Mexican imports with a 35 percent tariff. The United States imports $294.7 billion from Mexico, nearly as much as from China. Trump's tariffs would increase prices of the manufactured products, fruits, vegetables, coffee, and cotton we import from Mexico. Tariffs would benefit U.S. oil companies by raising prices on imported Mexican oil. By law, President Trump could only raise tariffs by 15 percent for 150 days without Congressional approval.

Trump advocates a protectionism that does not work in today's globally integrated economy. Other countries would retaliate, reducing American exports. It would also raise prices for American consumers. One reason for slow U.S. growth since the recession is that international trade hasn't rebounded. Tariffs and a trade war would only worsen that.

"Be the Greatest Job-Producing President in U.S. History"

Trump would have to create at least 21.5 million jobs to take that title. That's how many jobs President Clinton created in his eight years in office. That was a 19.6 percent increase. Trump would have to create at least 29.3 million jobs to beat that record.

Create jobs by eliminating outsourcing and bringing jobs back from Japan, China, and Mexico. Trump correctly identifies the problem. The U.S. lost 34 percent of its manufacturing jobs between 1998 and 2010. Many were outsourced by U.S. companies to save money. Others were eliminated by new technology, including robotics, artificial intelligence, and bio-engineering. Government-sponsored training for these specialties might create more jobs for U.S. workers than Trump›s trade war.

Keep the U.S. minimum wage where it is so U.S. companies can compete. The dollar rose 25 percent since 2014. That automatically makes U.S. workers 25 percent more expensive than those in India, Mexico, and other countries whose currencies have fallen. Since China›s currency is fixed to the dollar, its labor costs have also gone up 25 percent. Although this situation is temporary, it is still a bigger drag on U.S. competitiveness than raising the minimum wage. The U.S. minimum wage is $7.25 an hour, although many states with higher cost-of-living have mandated a higher wage. Ireland, the UK, Australia, and six European Union countries have a higher minimum wage than the United States.

Spend $1 trillion to rebuild U.S. infrastructure. That's $100 billion a year for ten years to repair America's aging roads, bridges, and airports. That's more than Obama's Economic Stimulus Plan, which spent $261 billion in four years on shovel-ready projects. Construction is the most efficient use of federal dollars to create jobs. A U Mass/Amherst study found that one billion dollars spent on public works created 19,795 jobs. That's better than defense spending, which created 8,555 for the same amount.

The U.S. jobs report is not a real number. The true unemployment rate is 18 percent, not 5 percent. The real unemployment rate includes those who are marginally attached or discouraged and part-time workers who would prefer full-time jobs. As of February 2016, that rate was 9.9 percent, not the widely-reported 4.9 percent. The worst real unemployment rate was 16.7 percent in January 2010, compared to 9.8 percent for the widely-reported rate. The real unemployment rate is typically double the widely-reported current unemployment rate.

Reduce regulations that restrict business growth. Ask federal departments for a list of wasteful regulations to be eliminated. Issue a temporary moratorium on new regulations. Cancel all executive orders. Eliminate Waters of the U.S. Rule and Clean Power Plan. The National Association of Manufacturers said that industry regulations cost $180 billion a year. Its studies show that U.S. manufacturing costs are 20 percent higher than other countries. (NAM wants to expand, not end, free trade agreements.) Trump named Steve Muchin to be his U.S. Treasury Secretary. He promised to loosen Dodd-Frank regulations that prevent banks from lending to small businesses. He said the Volcker Rule is too complicated.

"Reduce the Debt by Growing the Economy 6 Percent"

Grow the economy by 6 percent annually to increase tax revenues. That's too fast for healthy economic growth. It would create inflation, a boom-bust cycle, and then a crash.

Reduce the debt by eliminating waste and redundancy in federal spending. Trump demonstrated this in his campaign by using Twitter instead of expensive PR campaign. His emphasis on finding ways to contain the costs is one of his strategies outlined in his book *The Art of the Deal*.

Borrow knowing that if the economy crashed, you could make a deal. U.S. will never default because you can print the money. These are the most dangerous statements Trump has uttered. The first one is blatantly untrue. If the economy collapsed, there would be no one to make a deal with. It would send the dollar into a collapse. That would send the entire world into another Great Depression. The second comment would send the dollar back into decline. Interest rates would rise as creditors lost faith in U.S. Treasuries. That would create a recession.

Conclusion

Thank you again for downloading President Trump: How Donald Trump's Proposed Policies will Shape the USA and World in 2017 and Beyond! I hope you enjoyed reading it!

One thing you can derive from each of Trump's positions and policies, is that they tend to have quite a positive and profitable motive. Even though some positions may seem that they signify a personal gain, they still seem to be positive when portrayed in the view of the general public. However, if you dwell into the subtle details and the whole-scale implementation of his policies, they tend to breed a significant imbalance in the long-run stability of the subsequent relative fields of the policies. Some do tend to signify a haunting aspect; especially the international policies, but the domestic policies seem to have a positive outlook. The tax policies as well as concentration of integral problems like infrastructure and jobs might give Trump a positive reputable incentive.

While this detail outlook on Trump's policies and their expected affects provide a look into his Presidential tenure, Trump's uncertain position on some of the positions might change how the results of his policies turn out. Most Presidents, when informed and briefed about certain aspects and issues regarding their policies, seem to amend aspects and change their position on the issue. And with the unpredictability he has shown, anything can be expected, from the 44th President of the United States of America, Mr. Donald J. Trump.